In the
Dark Streets
Shineth

In the
Dark Streets
Shineth

❦ ❦ ❦

A 1941
CHRISTMAS EVE
STORY

David
McCullough

SHADOW
MOUNTAIN®

Visit us at ShadowMountain.com

Library of Congress Cataloging-in-Publication Data
McCullough, David G.
  In the dark streets shineth : a 1941 Christmas Eve story / David McCullough.
      p. cm.
  Includes bibliographical references.
  ISBN 978-1-60641-831-4 (hardbound : alk. paper)
  1. World War, 1939–1945—United States. 2. Christmas.
3. Roosevelt, Franklin D. (Franklin Delano), 1882–1945.
4. Churchill, Winston, 1874–1965. 5. Redner, Lewis H., 1831–1908.
O little town of Bethlehem. 6. Kent, Walter, 1911–1994. I'll be home for Christmas. I. Title.
  D811.M3963 2010
  940.53 ' 73—dc22   2010017585

Printed in the United States of America
Worzalla Book Manufacturing, Stevens Point, Wisconsin

10   9   8   7   6   5   4   3   2   1

$\mathcal{F}$OR THE LAST DECADE, the Mormon Tabernacle Choir and Orchestra at Temple Square have presented a Christmas concert as their gift to the community. Enjoyed by more than 80,000 concertgoers, the concert has been shared with the nation annually since 2004 on PBS television. Our renowned guest artists for these concerts have included Angela Lansbury, Audra McDonald, Frederica von Stade, Bryn Terfel, Renée Fleming, Brian Stokes Mitchell, Walter Cronkite, Peter Graves, Claire Bloom, and Edward K. Herrmann.

In 2009, I was thrilled when author and historian David McCullough accepted our invitation—extended to him through Utah businessman Larry H. Miller and his wife, Gail—to join with Natalie Cole as our

Christmas concert guests. I had known Mr.
McCullough through his Pulitzer Prize–
winning books, and his voice was familiar to
me as the narrator for many specials, notably
PBS's *American Experience*.

It was a pleasure to collaborate with
this man of such personal and professional
integrity. He brought a wonderful historical
perspective on American Christmas memories
with the touching stories behind the songs
"O Little Town of Bethlehem" (his mother's
favorite) and "I'll Be Home for Christmas."
I was honored to write the musical
accompaniment, built around these songs,

that underscored McCullough's retelling of the story of the Christmas 1941 visit of Prime Minister Winston Churchill as he met with President Franklin D. Roosevelt. The audience listened raptly as Mr. McCullough narrated this inspiring story of how the words of two great world leaders strengthened and uplifted an entire nation during a time of uncertainty.

As David McCullough shared with us, every song has a story, and Christmas is richer when we can share with family and friends those songs and those stories.

We are grateful to Mr. McCullough for joining us for this special holiday experience and hope that this book and the accompanying DVD can help recreate this special feeling of Christmas for you. ❧

MACK WILBERG,
MORMON TABERNACLE CHOIR,
MUSIC DIRECTOR

DOWN STAIRS FOR
INCOMING
TRAINS

INCOMING TRAINS

PENN STATION, NEW YORK CITY, 1941.

THE WHITE HOUSE.

ROOSEVELT FAMILY CHRISTMAS
AT THE WHITE HOUSE, 1941

USIC IS A

PART OF OUR HISTORY. ❧ IT

IS AN EXPRESSION OF WHO

WE ARE AND THE TIMES

WE'VE KNOWN, OUR HIGHS,

OUR LOWS, AND SO MUCH

THAT WE LOVE. ❧ TAKE AWAY

AMERICAN MUSIC FROM THE

AMERICAN STORY AND YOU

TAKE AWAY A GOOD PART OF

THE SOUL OF THE STORY. ❧

IMPOSSIBLE to imagine life
in America without it—without
"Shenandoah," or "Amazing
Grace," or "The Battle Hymn
of the Republic." Or Gershwin
or Copland or Scott Joplin. ❧

Or the music of Christmas in
America. ❧

I would like to tell you the
story of two classic American
Christmas carols—two of my
favorites—that both figured in
one of the darkest times ever,
during the Second World War.

❧ ❧ ❧

SHORTLY before Christmas 1941, Prime Minister Winston Churchill, at considerable personal risk, crossed the Atlantic in great secrecy to meet with President Franklin D. Roosevelt. ❧

PRESIDENT *Franklin D. Roosevelt (center)*
greeted Prime Minister Winston Churchill
(left) at the White House just after the
Prime Minister arrived in Washington, D.C.
on December 22, 1941.

On Christmas Eve, from a balcony at the White House, the two leaders spoke to a crowd of 20,000 gathered in the twilight. As reported in the *Washington Post*, "A crescent moon hung overhead. To the southward loomed the Washington Monument . . . as the sun dipped . . . behind the Virginia hills." ❧

President Roosevelt pressed a
button to light the Christmas tree.
Then he spoke to the crowd, and
by radio the world was listening. ❧

"Our strongest weapon in this
war," he said, "is that conviction
of the dignity and brotherhood
of man which Christmas Day
signifies." ❧

---

*In 1941, the site of the National Christmas
Tree was moved, at President Roosevelt's
request, from the Ellipse to the South Lawn
of the White House.*

PRESIDENT Roosevelt and
Prime Minister Churchill at the
Christmas Eve Celebration, 1941.
(Image taken from still frame of film.)

CHURCHILL began his remarks.
Here he was, he said, far from his own
country, far from his family. "Yet I cannot truthfully say that I feel far from
home," he told the hushed throng. ⸗

*Prime Minister Churchill and President
Roosevelt at a White House press conference,
December 23, 1941.*

"Here, in the midst of war, raging
and roaring over all the lands and
seas, creeping nearer to our hearts
and homes, here, amid all the
tumult, we have tonight the peace
of the spirit in each cottage home
and in every generous heart. . . .
Here, then, for one night only,
each home . . . should be a brightly-
lighted island of happiness and
peace." ❧

Christmas Eve Celebration at the Nation

Concert

UNITED STATES MARINE BAND

Captain William F. Santelmann, *Leader*
Henry Weber, *Second Leader*

PROGRAM

1. "BREAK FORTH, O BEAUTEOUS HEAVENLY LIGHT" from .... *Bach*
   "THE CHRISTMAS ORATORIO" ....
2. "THE HEAVENS ARE TELLING" from "THE CREATION" .... *Haydn*
3. "THE HEAVENS PRAISE THEE, ETERNAL KING" .... *Beethoven*
4. Fantasy: "CHRISTMAS MEMORIES" .... *Finck*
5. "HALLELUJAH CHORUS" from "THE MESSIAH" .... *Handel*
   CAROL BY MASSED CHORISTERS

   "JOY TO THE WORLD" .... *Handel*

Arrival of the President and His Party
5:00 P. M.

INVOCATION .... His Excellency, The Most Reverend Joseph Corrigan

INTRODUCTORY REMARKS .... Honorable Guy Mason
Commissioner of the District of Columbia

Greetings

OF THE PEOPLE OF WASHINGTON TO THE
PRESIDENT AND MRS. ROOSEVELT

Presented by

Louella Boyd, Troop 95, Girl Scouts of the District of Columbia
J. Robert Thrower, Jr., Eagle Scout, Troop 104, Boy Scouts of National Capital Area
Council

Lighting of the Living Community Christmas Tree

By The
PRESIDENT OF THE UNITED STATES

Community Christmas Tree, 1941

The L

Christmas~sing merrilie

THE LIGHTING

OF THE

National

Community Christmas Tree

WASHINGTON, D. C.

Christmas Eve

WEDNESDAY, DECEMBER 24, 1941

THE WHITE HOUSE

Four-Thirty

Calv

St.

"ADESTE F

"IT CAME

"SILENT N

"CANTIQU

BENEDIC

THE PRINTED PROGRAM *for the* 1941 *Christmas Eve Celebration did not
mention Prime Minister Churchill because his visit was a closely guarded secret.*

T HE FOLLOWING morning,
Christmas Day, the Prime Minister
and the President went to church,

___

*L*EAVING THE WHITE HOUSE *for Christmas
services, December 25, 1941.* Left to right: *Eleanor
Roosevelt, Winston Churchill, Franklin D. Roosevelt,
General Edwin Watson.*

where with the congregation they joined in singing "O Little Town of Bethlehem," which Churchill had never heard before. ૮

The words of the hymn, one of the most beloved of Christmas carols, had been written long before by a famous American clergyman, Phillips Brooks, after a visit to the Holy Land.

૮ ૮ ૮

$\mathcal{P}$HILLIPS BROOKS *at age 27,*
three years before he wrote "O Little
Town of Bethlehem" (ca. 1862).

On Christmas Eve in Jerusalem in 1865, Brooks rode through the dark by horseback to the place above the town where, he was told, the shepherds had gathered with their sheep. ❧

"BETHLEHEM," STEEL ENGRAVING
by an anonymous artist (ca. 1850).

After returning to his church in Philadelphia, in an effort to put down on paper what he had felt that night, Brooks wrote a poem. ❧

O little town of Bethlehem
How still we see thee lie
Above thy deep & dreamless sleep
The silent stars go by
Yet in thy dark streets shineth
The Everlasting Light
The hopes & fears of all the years
Are met in thee tonight

𝓕ACSIMILE COPY OF THE *first stanza of "O Little Town of Bethlehem" in Phillips Brooks's handwriting.*

A few days before Christmas 1868,
he asked the organist, Lewis
Redner, to put the poem to music,
that it might be sung at the
Christmas service. ❧

Redner tried but with no success.
He went to bed Christmas Eve
feeling he had utterly failed.
"My brain was all confused,"
he later said. "But I was roused
from sleep late in the night hearing
an angel-strain . . . and seizing a
piece of music paper I jotted down
the treble of the tune." ❧

CHURCHILL HAD spoken in his remarks from the White House balcony of every home as a "brightly-lighted island" in the dark. In the first stanza of "O Little Town of Bethlehem" is the line, "Yet in thy dark streets shineth the everlasting Light." ❧

I like to think of Churchill and Roosevelt singing that line in particular. And, as would be said of the Prime Minister, he always sang lustily, if not exactly in tune.

❧ ❧ ❧

$\mathcal{F}$OLLOWING CHURCH SERVICES, *the*
Prime Minister and President Roosevelt
greet the daughter of the pastor of
Christ Church.

By 1942, with the war still raging, more than 1,000,000 Americans were serving overseas, in sixty-five parts of the world, and it was with those men and women and their families in mind that two talented New Yorkers, lyricist Kim Gannon and composer Walter Kent, went to work on a new Christmas song. ❧

A YOUNG BRIDE *bids farewell to her soldier*

husband at Penn Station in New York City.

Walter Kent had already composed "The White Cliffs of Dover," which had become nearly an anthem in Britain. Now they wrote "I'll Be Home for Christmas," which in simplest terms expressed the longing for home and light in the darkness felt by so many. ❧

"I'll be home for Christmas,
where the love-light gleams,

I'll be home for Christmas,
if only in my dreams." ❧

When recorded by Bing Crosby
in 1943, the song became the most
popular carol of the era, even more
than "White Christmas."

ど ど ど

$\mathcal{H}$ISTORY CAN be a great

source of strength and affirmation,

and especially in difficult, dangerous

times. And the words and music

we love, and that have stood the

test of time, mean still more when

we know their story.

❧ ❧ ❧

$\mathscr{F}$ranklin D. Roosevelt
Christmas Eve Message, 1941

❦ ❦ ❦

$\mathscr{F}$ELLOW WORKERS FOR FREEDOM:

There are many men and women in America—sincere and faithful men and women—who are asking themselves this Christmas:

How can we light our trees? How can we give our gifts? How can we meet and worship with love and with uplifted spirit and heart in a world at war, a world of fighting and suffering and death?

How can we pause, even for a day, even for Christmas Day, in our urgent labor of arming a decent humanity against the enemies which beset it?

How can we put the world aside, as men and women put the world aside in peaceful years, to rejoice in the birth of Christ?

These are natural—inevitable—questions in every part of the world which is resisting the evil thing.

And even as we ask these questions, we know the answer. There is another preparation demanded of this nation beyond and beside the preparation of weapons and materials of war. There is demanded also of us the preparation of our hearts; the arming of our hearts. And when we make ready our hearts for the labor and the suffering and the ultimate victory which lie ahead, then we observe Christmas Day—with all of its memories and all of its meanings—as we should.

Looking into the days to come, I have set aside a Day of Prayer, and in that Proclamation I have said:

"The year 1941 has brought upon our nation a war of aggression by powers dominated by arrogant rulers whose selfish purpose is to destroy free institutions. They would thereby take from the freedom-loving peoples of the earth the hard-won liberties gained over many centuries.

"The new year of 1942 calls for the courage and the resolution of old and young to help to win a world struggle in order that we may preserve all that we hold dear.

"We are confident in our devotion to country, in our love of freedom, in our inheritance of courage. But our strength, as the strength of all men everywhere, is of greater avail as God upholds us.

"Therefore, I . . . do hereby appoint the first day of the year 1942 as a day of prayer, of asking forgiveness for our shortcomings of the past, of consecration to the tasks of the present, of asking God's help in days to come.

"We need His guidance that this people may be humble in spirit but strong in the conviction of the right; steadfast to endure sacrifice, and brave to achieve a victory of liberty and peace."

Our strongest weapon in this war is that conviction of the dignity and brotherhood of man which Christmas Day signifies—more than any other day or any other symbol.

Against enemies who preach the principles of hate and practice them, we set our faith in human love and in God's care for us and all men everywhere.

It is in that spirit, and with particular thoughtfulness of those, our sons and brothers, who serve in our armed forces on land and sea, near and far—those who serve for us and endure for us—that we light our Christmas candles now across the continent from one coast to the other on this Christmas Eve.

We have joined with many other nations and peoples in a very great cause. Millions of them have been engaged in the task of defending good with their life-blood for months and for years.

One of their great leaders stands beside me. He and his people in many parts of the world are having their Christmas trees with their little children around them, just as we do here. He and his people have pointed the way in courage and in sacrifice for the sake of little children everywhere.

And so I am asking my associate, my old and good friend, to say a word to the people of America, old and young, tonight—Winston Churchill, Prime Minister of Great Britain.

❧ ❧ ❧

WINSTON CHURCHILL
CHRISTMAS EVE MESSAGE, 1941

꙳ ꙳ ꙳

SPEND THIS ANNIVERSARY and festival far from my country, far from my family, yet I cannot truthfully say that I feel far from home. Whether it be the ties of blood on my mother's side, or the friendships I have developed here over many years of active life, or the commanding sentiment of comradeship in the common cause of great peoples who speak the same language, who kneel at the same altars, and to a very large extent, pursue the same ideals, I cannot feel myself a stranger here in the centre and at the summit of the United States. I feel a sense of unity and fraternal association which, added to the kindliness of your welcome, convinces me that I have a right to sit at your fireside and share your Christmas joys.

This is a strange Christmas Eve. Almost the whole world is locked in deadly struggle, and, with the most terrible weapons which science can devise, the nations advance upon each other. Ill would it be for us this Christmastide if we were not sure that no greed for the land or wealth of any other people, no vulgar ambition, no morbid lust for material gain at the expense of others, had led us to the field. Here, in the midst of war, raging and roaring over all the lands and seas, creeping nearer to our hearts and homes, here, amid all the tumult, we have tonight the peace of the spirit in each cottage home and in every generous heart. Therefore we may cast aside for this night at least the cares and dangers which beset us, and make for the children an evening of happiness in a world of storm. Here, then, for one night only, each home throughout the English-speaking world should be a brightly-lighted island of happiness and peace.

Let the children have their night of fun and laughter. Let the gifts of Father Christmas delight their play. Let us grown-ups share to the full in their unstinted pleasures before we turn again to the stern task and the formidable years that lie before us, resolved that, by our sacrifice and daring, these same children shall not be robbed of their inheritance or denied their right to live in a free and decent world.

And so, in God's mercy, a happy Christmas to you all.

ĕ ĕ ĕ

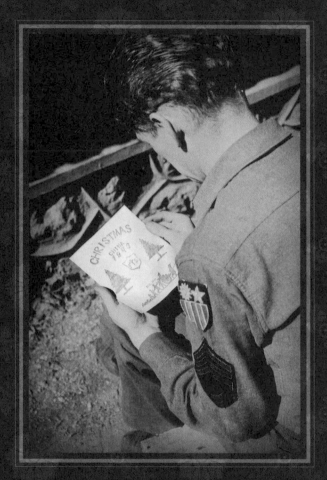

A U.S. serviceman in China,
Christmas, 1943.

Near Ederen, Germany, December 1944.

SOME OF THE SIXTEEN MILLION AMERICANS WHO SERVED
IN THE U.S. ARMED FORCES DURING WORLD WAR II.

CHRISTMAS EVE IN AMERICA, CA. 1940S.

Homeward bound on the USS *Yorktown*,
Manila, Philippines, 1946.

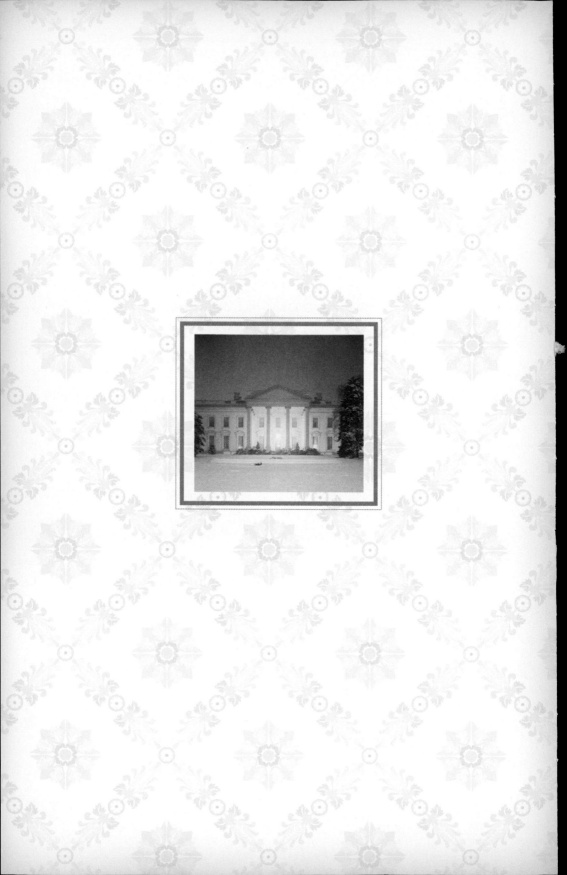

Photo Credits

ξ ξ ξ

Front cover: Franklin D. Roosevelt and Winston Churchill. Courtesy of the Franklin D. Roosevelt Library and Museum website; version date 2009.

Back cover: © Schenectady Museum; Hall of Electrical History Foundation/CORBIS.

Page vi: Mormon Tabernacle Choir.

Page viii: © H. Armstrong Roberts/CORBIS.

Page ix: © Bettmann/CORBIS.

Page x: © Philip Gendreau/Bettmann/CORBIS.

Page xi: Library of Congress, Washington, D.C.

Page xii: Time Life Pictures/Time & Life Pictures/Getty Images.

Page xiii: Roosevelt Family Christmas at the White House, 1941. Courtesy of the Franklin D. Roosevelt Library and Museum website; version date 2009.

Page 3: Library of Congress, Washington, D.C.

Page 4: Franklin D. Roosevelt and Winston Churchill, Washington, D.C., December 22, 1941. Courtesy of the Franklin D. Roosevelt Library and Museum website; version date 2009.

Page 7: © 1940 The Associated Press.

❧ ❧ ❧